Above the Fall Line

poems by

Clara Silverstein

Finishing Line Press
Georgetown, Kentucky

Above the Fall Line

In memory of Mary Jean Irion (1922-2019)

Copyright © 2025 by Clara Silverstein
ISBN 979-8-88838-880-8 First Edition
All rights reserved under International and Pan-American Copyright Conventions. No part of this book may be reproduced in any manner whatsoever without written permission from the publisher, except in the case of brief quotations embodied in critical articles and reviews.

Publisher: Leah Huete de Maines
Editor: Christen Kincaid
Cover Art: Clara Silverstein—James River in Richmond, Virginia
Author Photo: Daniel Nystedt, Nystedt Photography
Cover Design: Elizabeth Maines McCleavy

Order online: www.finishinglinepress.com
also available on amazon.com

Author inquiries and mail orders:
Finishing Line Press
PO Box 1626
Georgetown, Kentucky 40324
USA

Contents

PART I

Tourist in My Hometown 1
Richmond's Canal Walk 2
Tour of Capitol Square 3
After Richmond Burned in 1865 4
Whitewash on Concrete Walls 5
I Try to Learn German 6
Origin Story 7
High School Reunion 8
Running the Richmond Marathon, 2006 9

PART II

School Desegregation, 1970s 13
Segregated Swimming Pool 14
Visiting the Confederate Trenches 15
The First Busing Year 16
History Class
    i. The Only White Girl 17
    ii. I Imagine the Early Days of the Massachusetts Bay Colony 18
    iii. If I Were Pocahontas Posing For My Portrait 19
    iv. To Bake Apples, 1760 20
    v. Antebellum Biscuits 21
    vi. I Imagine Abraham Lincoln Visiting Richmond 22
    vii. Field Trip 23
The Way to School 24
Cousins 25
Eighth Grade Bathroom 26
Watching the Popular Kids 27
Police Search 28
Sex Ed, 10th Grade 29
Older Boy 30
Standard Drug Store 31
Telling on My Sister 32
Family History 33
The Starving Time 34
In My Dark Days 35
Cinderella Envy 36
Waiting for the World to Take Back its Colors 37
Lake Anna 38
Tourists at the World Trade Center, 1976 39
In the James River 40
Driving 41

PART III

Ambrotype 45
Grandfather's Lost Mansion 46
Uncle Ed 47
Mother as a Young Woman.. 48
Maymont Park, 1961.. 49
Kiddie Pool, 1965 50
Father's Last Photo of His Girls 51
Mother as a Widow 52
Swings at Humphrey Calder Park... 53
Photo Booth, 1974 55

PART IV

Second Time Around 59
Urgent Spring 60
How We Meet 61
Amplified, My Son's Heart at 12 Weeks 62
Out to Buy Milk 63
Twigs for Mother... 64
Truth About Death.. 65
I Imagine My Son Leaving Home 66
After My Mother's Hysterectomy... 67
My Father's Hometown 68
Loss 69
Father's Day... 70

PART V

Why Did You Move to Boston?... 73
Where I Raised My Children... 74
Outside the Boston Marathon Bomber Trial 75
Home, Shutdown... 76
Making a Mask with My Mother's Sewing Kit 77
I Couldn't Protect My Sister... 78
Elegy for My Father 79
After Visiting My Mother's Memorial Bench.. 80
A Calm Place 81
April Storm 82
May Walk 83
On the Anniversary of My Father's Death 84

Acknowledgments... 85
Bio... 87

PART I

Tourist in My Hometown

when my mother puts my childhood
home in Richmond on the market, I return
to wander the lawn, magnolia blossoms
littered like crushed coffee cups

at the apartments under construction
in weeds near the Esso station,
where my best friend and I wriggled
under the chain link fence after men

left for the day, tiptoed up plywood stairs
to framed rooms, where we fingered idle
drills, table saws, nail guns,
blew smoke rings out roughed-in

windows, spied on everything
we would leave at the houses below—
the wire weave of porch screens
sieving the glow of television

families sparring and guffawing,
everything we wanted
in the humming edges
where the floodlights died away.

Richmond's Canal Walk

Shockoe leads to a low place—
cobblestones, moss, rumble
of moving water. Towpath shadowed
by one wall from the Haxall Mill.
Night and day, it ground flour
flung into barrels, last load
on the Danville train. No solace
in light-flecked water,
just the gray sighs of Sunday
cars heading across a river
still clogged with stone piers
from a bridge Rebels burned
in early April. The shard
of glass I pick up: remnant
of a window exploded
when the city fell, or a stranger's
fifth of gin? I move one way,
the fragments shift.
Move again. Another view.

Tour of Capitol Square

From this height, the guide says, *Richmonders could see
blue troops worming up through streets*

burned when the city fell in 1865—boots pummeling ashes,
burdened wagons creaking. *Yankees took it all*—

smoldering tobacco, smashed barrels,
gutters of whiskey, this grass on the hill.

Refugees huddled in tablecloths, sacks,
as broad stripes and bright stars

spurted above *the business district,
nothing left* but a pall of smoke and rubble.

After Richmond Burned in 1865

My great-grandfather saw the sun
rise, red as a welt
over charred brick
facade of a ruined mill,
windows gaping like eye sockets
above a business district
that would be rebuilt to sweep him in,
black hat in hands, at the unveiling
of Confederate statues.

He put a Rebel flag in his lapel
to trade with the wounded and the proud
until the Depression spit out his business,
sent him off the third-story balcony,
and my grandfather, shame-faced,
to the tobacco factory,
his breath an ember in his throat.

In World War II, my mother stirred rationed sugar
into her tea—the bag always re-used—
with monogrammed silver spoons
left over from prosperity.

At my school, in the asphalt heat
of the playground, girls told me, *get lost,*
so I ran past camellia bushes
into my mother's yard overgrown,
at supper every night, her face like concrete;
across the Huguenot Bridge, the metal railing where I fell
in love with the roar and vertigo of the James River;
past the dance hall where I skulked in the raucousness
after my boyfriend left, wandered Broad Street,
chicken and ribs joints, vacant
lots where I wove through cones in driver's ed
until I learned enough to speed
away, camshaft churning
everything slammed inside my car,
heading north.

Whitewash on Concrete Walls

My great-grandmother disembarked in Baltimore,
mouth pinched above a lace collar,
hungry for a new language.
I was given her name
and only one word of her native tongue:
Nein!

This is her world sealed off:
whitewash on concrete walls,
a bakery, a fabric store, a sanitarium,
the lake shaped like a feather,
hills of Württemberg humped to the horizon.
Cousins in the cemetery,
Geboren, gestorben, Jewish star,
Hebrew prayer—
their synagogue torched on *Kristallnacht.*

I Try to Learn German

I've lost the texture of my ancestral
tongue—meandering vowels pushed
aside by declarations: *ach, so, gut*

a prickly novelty like hazelnut
torte nibbled with a torrent
of coffee, rat-a-tat greetings

every word I learn trapped
behind my lipstick, a brazen and false front—
I got away from the precision

of third pronouns that have no gender,
nouns that glom onto each other
through *Wortbildung* like Jenga

blocks and scarves loop-de-looping;
trains that must run on schedule.

Origin Story

    (after Terrance Hayes)

I'm the daughter of a wise man
and a crone. Before the wasteland
of olive carpet, there was a fringed
blanket, a butterfly night light, stories
before bed. God summoned the wise man
to heaven while I jumped
rope in the street. *Sea shells, cockle bells,*
I sang, while he curled himself
into clouds. Then there were stale
crackers, an empty thermos, no more
picnics. Now I come from a chain
link fence and four lanes
of traffic. I come from home
alone in low temperatures, a room that needs
yellow. I will not listen to the pennies
pinched to suffocation. I come
blessed with a giggle and curls.
Yesterday, I put on flip flops, short
shorts, took myself to the corner
store, counted the honks from men
as if they were precious coins.

High School Reunion

Faces hover like fake Tiffany,
orange and brown shards factory glued,
bad taste in the seventies—
all aboard Grand Funk Railroad,
chug-a-lug this and toke that,
don't trust anyone, not even the President.

Under the bleachers with boys, I fumbled
shame that never scrubbed away,
body a scrap heap clanking
past the friend who fed me
snow ice cream with maple syrup,
another whose tropical fishtank rescued me
from my mother's pathological drabness;

always I ended up choosing the boy
who made me feel like winter
trees garlanded with lights
until he walked away
and I came unstrung.

Running the Richmond Marathon, 2006

We're off, Kenyans first along Broad Street,
past taverns with blacked-out windows, discount shoes,
department stores closed to make way for condos.
Today nervous runners like me with jagged gait,
ease into the breathing, the practiced pace
measured in minutes per mile, step and breathe,
one mile after another, and here comes Arthur Ashe
racket raised, for years unheralded
in his hometown, turned away.
Now my mother's high school, Dixie at assemblies,
lunches packed by maids
giving way to kids strutting like Superfly
among hippie wanna-bes, daisies threading their jeans.
Time to cross the river, fatigue and heat
fading the skyline,
banks and warehouses stacked like blocks,
a landscape I could rearrange
with the sweep of one sweaty hand—
back to the beginning, a bluff
above the fall line of the James—
but I keep following the arrows,
the mile signs,
metronome feet,
time collapsing
into an arch of balloons,
I can get there—
move ahead—
I can cross that line.

PART II

School Desegregation, 1970s

> *What's Going On*
> —Marvin Gaye

Volume dialed up from scratchy
transistors on the playground, we dance

The Hustle. Teachers huddle by the door, too tired
of their jobs to reprimand us. Nobody cares

what we do as long as we don't fight. Maybe
one day we will leave this weed-choked

asphalt. *You know we've got to find a way—*
a reckoning is coming.

Segregated Swimming Pool

This is the only place allowed for kids
Mother teaches, who ricochet around the baby pool
in underwear because, she whispers,
nobody buys them bathing suits.

Maybe Mother is too busy handing out school
towels or herding four-year-olds through the sprinkler
to notice we're the only ones with flat hair and pale arms
inside the fence, and I'm the only 11-year-old,

bored enough to take barefoot steps toward the adult
pool, where everyone falls silent, staring from towels
laid flat on concrete,
while I weave through, feet and face burning

this stifling August day. I don't
belong the way I do at the country club
where my grandfather plays golf, where I passed
the lifeguard's deep water test,

practiced swan dives. I climb
the board today: up the ladder, step, two, three,
along the non-skid length, jump, soar,
in the armor of my tank suit, point toes, plunge.

Visiting the Confederate Trenches

After school, my friends and I spurred
        stick horses down Dead Man's trench,
                the afternoon of Virginia History

rushing past as our teacher unfolded
        her grandfather's powder-scorched flag
                laid it across scarred desks, voice quavering,

setting us straight about breastworks gouged
        from mud, the noble, shivering soldiers
                shoeless, on half-rations, lying low as Yankees prowled.

We made the younger kids
        be Indians who whooped and beat
                puny fists against their chests

while we galloped off to strategize
        behind a curtain of vines,
                silence falling like a tent flap

as we loaded up on ammo,
        sun-warmed, old stones
                sagging in our pockets.

The First Busing Year

Hey, Tiger, Sparky, Hot Stuff,
    friends yelled to each other in the halls
        but never spoke to me.

I wisped along, gauzy face under hair
    so straight girls sneaked up for a stroke,
        as if something good might rub off.

I insulated myself in silence so thick
    their nails never penetrated.
        Only the teachers called my name.

Clock hands became my compass,
    needling the minutes each day
        until the bus sputtered up to the curb.

I looked forward to the thwack
    of my bookbag against vinyl,
        my shoulder sometimes bumping

Liz, who didn't flinch,
    hummed pop tunes,
        passed me gum, let me sag.

History Class

i. The Only White Girl

On film strip days,
lights off and shades pulled
against the day's glare,

I turned sideways in my seat,
inched my hand across the pencil
groove on my desk.

The narrator droned on
about Betsy Ross, clever seamstress
of our nation's first flag,

holding out
for five-pointed stars,
though George Washington wanted six—

I reached for the boy in front
of me, slid my books
to hide our twined fingers.

When the lights when went on
and everyone blinked, oblivious,
I wanted to take shears to white

cloth, cut stars of my own,
make a banner for the nation I lived in.

ii. I Imagine the Early Days of the Massachusetts Bay Colony

Wilderness: brackish
marshes. English axes, saws.

Gangplanks. Beasts
of burden unloaded to break

raw land. City chopped out
from a swamp. Gospel

forced. Trades of
corn for beads. Fields

fenced. Hunter-
gatherers turned

trespassers. Rivers
dammed, renamed.

Smallpox blankets.
Rum. Removal.

The King: a villain
impeding progress.

New nation:
sanctity and thirst.

iii. If I Were Pocahontas Posing for My Portrait

England, 1616

This ruff and bodice too tight
        against my breath. I've already curtseyed

for King James, already alighted from coaches
        at masques and entertainments:

hey, ho, the wind and the rain
        for the rain it raineth every day.

I need to quell impatience while the artist takes
        my measure, his mouth a purse,

marsh-colored eyes foolish
        as the feather in the hat

he pushed onto my head
        to hide the dark flood

of my hair. He thinks I'm no
        fair lady, but my neck

grows thick as a root,
        upholds me under this brim,

curled like the tip of a wave
        on the return crossing I hasten to make.

iv. To Bake Apples, 1760

From the barrel down
cellar, choose a Rome
Beauty. Anoint
each slice with a store
of sweet butter.
Strew sugar upon it,
a good thickness. A quarter
of nutmeg, grated.
Roll the crust. Wet
the edges. Crimp.

Inhale the dear
scent. Try not to ache
for back home across
the heave of water.
Give thanks for the harvest,
an orchard red and gold.

Take the pie down
the lane, past thorn
bushes etched with frost,
give it to your neighbor.

v. Antebellum Biscuits

Add kindling to the cookstove,
watch flames flare,

feed them carefully.
Bowl, spoon, flour tin.

A handful of flour, another.
Let the fire hiss.

Cut and cut the butter.
Squeeze, release.

Eggs crack and splash.
Spoon explodes yolks.

Round, round until
everything masses together.

Dough flung on the countertop.
Glass jar stamping circles.

Spit for good measure.

vi. I Imagine Abraham Lincoln Visiting Richmond

April 1865

The city fallen,
stunned. Ladies in black
turn threadbare
backs to the President,

who rushes his Union
escorts into the Jefferson Davis
house just abandoned
to soldiers who swarm settees.

Lincoln jams unsteady legs
under the desk, while his son leans in
for the pen, signs his name
on a blank sheet, flourish on the L,

rests one arm, light
as a scarf on the careworn
cloth of his father's collar—
the President pleased

until grimness takes
its customary roost.
Outside, ashes rain,
smoke sticks in every throat.

vii. Field Trip

My white face a boulder
too heavy for even the nicest
kids in class to try lifting
on the school bus, so I huff

against the cold window,
tracing hearts with a forefinger
on fog, bangs across my eyes
like drawn curtains.

Everyone jostling,
two and three to a seat, Sly
and the Family Stone crackling
from a radio in a coat pocket,

everyone jiving
until Mr. Freeman stands,
palms forward,
Y'all hush up, now!

At the Malvern Hill battlefield,
I stand ashamed among the others,
bones smoothed over,
grass sown, then mowed.

The Way to School

I press dense books
against my breasts,

new and overgrown.
Nobody I like

ever likes me back.
As I pass the construction

site, men hoot.
Rude laughter

showers like sparks
from welding,

expressway thundering
under my skirt.

I have no choice
but to cross their bridge.

Cousins

Downpour! We dash inside
for bikinis held together with strings,

hollering as we run out into it,
barefoot down Monument Avenue,

spray of puddles, the honk
a surprise. *Hey, girlies,*

a man's head out the window,
tongue like the tail of a cat,

rain beating down on us,
penned up traffic at the light.

Eighth Grade Bathroom

My face stubbed out like a cigarette.
Kool pack taps the wall.
A match flares.
Menthol smoke blurs the room.

Kool pack taps the wall.
Girls comb Afros with picks.
Menthol smoke blurs the room.
I can't find my face in the mirror.

Girls comb Afros with picks.
Lipstick twists in its gold sheath.
I can't find my face in the mirror.
Laughter flits across tile.

Lipstick twists in its gold sheath.
Exhale.
Laughter flits across tile.
The stall too flimsy.

Exhale.
A match flares.
The stall too flimsy.
My face stubbed out like a cigarette.

Watching the Popular Kids

Lots of room for the loud hiss
of sodas opening, and the girl
who exhales smoke, lifting her long neck,
top and jeans hugging her swagger
for the boy with glasses
tinted the color of rainclouds.

Their flirting has nothing to do
with me, though I know how to pair off
somewhere else, at the cotillion,
white gloves turning sweating hands
genteel, an unfamiliar fist in the small of my back,
heels unmoored from the waltz.

I wear my blouse like a tarp
at a construction site, secretly
hammering myself
into proper posture, nailing
the inflections *yes ma'am, no ma'am
thank you kindly*, until I can pass.

Police Search

The stranger in my yard smiles, ducks, leaves
        the back gate gaping, could have
              let the dog out,
    but she is inside, barking.

An officer in too-bright shoes
        knocks, clears his throat,
            sorry to trouble you, ma'am
    on the run, a rapist, *have you seen…?*

I would never tell that officer,
        never tell Mother, who shakes
            her head, goes back to sudsing
    supper dishes.

He was so agile
        as he scaled our fence,
            toed each chain link,
    reached and twisted,

leaped over
        into the territory of lost
            wiffle balls, tree forts
    armed with acorns.

Sex Ed, 10th Grade

The teacher doesn't tell us how
to feel. She calmly points out erogenous
zones on a diagram, one male, one female.

I wasn't expecting the underarms,
or such matter-of-fact delivery
from a slim, 26-year-old divorcee.

We have to find sex partners
on our own. I don't want boys
in the class, who know too much,

or the others—goof-balls,
partiers hopped up on six-packs,
the married neighbor

out by his garage, cigarette
smoke barely veiling his leer.
Nobody knows I panic

when undressed near others, head
an airplane over clouds of skin.
Here are the controls: diaphragms, pills,

condoms unrolled on a plastic penis.
Don't trust withdrawal, or Coke douche.
If all fails, there's the clinic.

The teacher drives us on a field trip,
tells us to ignore those fanatics
out front, their chants and gruesome posters.

It's legal now, we have the right
to the metal table, stirrups, aspirator,
antiseptic instead of alleys.

Older Boy

        Already a senior, car keys
spinning around his finger,
       one eyebrow inching up
   as I balance a cigarette
            on the edge of his ashtray—
    in the Camaro
his tongue a whirligig,
      breath hollowing me out.

      What he offers, I want,
only not now, not this way;
           I'm afraid to lose
       the filigree
of streets paved with hidden
           shards of brightness

           the two of us flinging ourselves
at each other, his face
            too rough,
   too close,
       my hands hammering
      no.

Standard Drug Store

Off the downtown bus, Broad Street,
men idling outside the newsstand,
sun glaring off asphalt, a buzzer

startles me into the store's cool hum,
lunch counter a gleaming relic,
stools removed from their metal poles,

juice dispensers shut down,
nobody can eat here,
nobody will renovate.

I duck past shelves of pink sponge
hair curlers and Afro-Sheen
to the feminine aisle, the birth control

I'm too embarrassed to buy
in my neighborhood. Here, I'm glad
the cashier would never tell on me,

though she can't help but notice
my teenage plans and precautions
while I wait for my change, the bag she hands back.

Telling On My Sister

We rode our bikes top speed
at one another, veering at the last second,
the almost crashes exhilarating.
Risk always gave us a charge.
After Father died, Mother's petty rules:
Switch off the lights.
Open the presents without tearing.
Re-use the wrapping paper.

We shoplifted our way through candy,
but I lagged behind her nonchalance,
her developing body, her narrowing eyes.
Soon there was no room
for me in her schemes.
She packed her Lonely
Planet guidebooks,
Mexican shawls, moved out,
found a boyfriend strong
enough to punch her back.

Family History

My sister beat me
by the piano. I knew loss
of breath and panic. My rib cage
held but trembled, like branches
in a gale. Our mother shook
her fist at me. I did not
get up. She said, *I will send you
to the dog house where you belong.* I ran
from her. She pushed me
onto the back porch. I wanted to be
a dog. It was winter in Virginia
and cold. My sister came out. *Now you're going
to get it, you brat.* I pushed her away
because I didn't know she needed
me. Inside, we were always yelling. *Fuck you*
was not allowed. I kicked
the door. Slunk back in and starved
myself until my bones grew sharp.

The Starving Time

I hammer a steel cage
around my hunger,
where it awaits, quivering, the handouts—
dry rolls, apple slices, cups of water.
I train my appetite toward the dirt,
a harvest of parsnips, beets, potatoes,
each dense as precious metal.

All winter, I change
crème brûlée into cotton, chocolate into mud—
an alchemy of resolve.
Lemon and strong Darjeeling
cleanse me.

Flesh sloughs off.
My stomach shrinks
like an old balloon;
my pelvis juts out
like a trophy:

I have triumphed
over everything oily, sweet, rich,
the cream at my center
vanquished—dried up
like a lake in a drought.

In My Dark Days

I throw my hunger out
with grass clippings,
coffee grounds, last year's leaves,
my determination to shrink
hardening into a mallet
that strikes my ribs
like a glockenspiel—
my whole body vibrating,
shaken loose, bones
gathered up in a drawstring bag
that nobody wants to carry.

Cinderella Envy

                    Isn't she lucky to meet someone
who takes instant delight in her silhouette, curlicues
of perfume on her wrists. Her buttons blaze
bright as buttercups while her breath rotates
into spun sugar.

                    All I want is one man
to notice me smoldering, hold me as I spin through
a waltz, even if he's looking over my shoulder,
eyeing someone glossier.

                    So smitten, her prince, she forgets
her feet are bound in glass and the clock unwinds.

Waiting for the World to Take Back its Colors

       green, a gouge
of hope with a black

       core, its rich
loam, territory of worms,

       volleying calls
of owls, mauve in the chill,

       before orange
stains the edges.

Lake Anna

Past the barricade
on the two-lane road,
we wade into the engineered
lake, its water still warm
from the reactor's
core. We lie back, let it
soak the sweat from our scalps,
buoy us as we backstroke
under a cobalt sky,
crickets clicking in low grass
like Geiger counters
on the brand-new shore
surrounded by acres
of sagging wires,
fields of meadowsweet, parched
where lines of corn once reached.

Tourists at the World Trade Center, 1976

In the metallic dark,
numbers flickered 90…100…110
until we stepped, jittery,
into the glass room,
Top of the World.

Over the rail, August
glazed rooftops and spires,
draped the Hudson
in haze—
Liberty, dulled.

Leaning in the circle
of his arms, his heart was a clock
against my ear, his chest
a pillar, I thought
behind me forever.

In the James River

My friend went down
        that spring in a haze,
                unseasonable air,
                        forsythia still unfurling.

Toni—the girl who tied her scarf
        around her Afro, ends
                draped across one shoulder,
                        that i in her name dotted with a heart.

When I came down for breakfast,
        the ambulance and grim policemen were there
                on the front page of the *Times-Dispatch,*
                        the clock face awash in grief....

I looked down at my toes, nail polish
        pink, garish in sandals
                with glued-on flowers
                        for the pool, so flimsy.

In my yearbook, she wrote, "I hope your life
        is very happy forever," the force
                she must have counted on as she stood,
                        slipped, gravity unrelenting.

Driving

I want to swerve
from the church
parking lot,
white arrows
directing the pattern,
roar down River
Road, swoop
and dip, open
up the wind,
pass rapids, rocks,
water fractured,
frantic pines,
staccato lines—
Mother in the passenger
seat, for once
silent,
her new blue
sedan blazing
past the city's crumbled
grandeur
outflanked by neon
food strips, Gas
N Go, outsized
subdivisions, plantations
turned touristy
in rampant outskirts
everything beyond
what she knows.

PART III

Ambrotype

At 17, Great-Grandpappy Tim, solemn in slouch
hat and gray shell jacket in the Carolinas

Campaign—unsparing path of Sherman.
Mustered out, he went back

to farming. My grandmother remembers
his whiskers, rough as unplaned wood.

Now I want to trace his part
of my story. I drive south out of snow

by a river named Tar. Downtown's a relic
from 1910. The road named after the family

leads to a trailer park in a parched field. Nobody
looks when I step from the car. I'm just

leaving, anyway, following the line
of march to Devil's Racetrack Road

where I scuff the dirt of heritage.

Grandfather's Lost Mansion

The century turned above the avenue
thrumming with autos, electricity,
bronze Rebel heroes, household retinue:
chauffeur, nursemaid, and cook for fripperies
at meals, monogrammed silver napkin rings.
He won golf trophies for unerring aim—
sound business sense, but blind to the wobbling
markets beneath his jovial acclaim

until the crash that snatched fortune away.
His mouth grew tight as he arranged to take
a factory job—tobacco dried and flayed.
Foreclosed, depressed, he flat refused to make
a spectacle, never apologized
as joy vanished with servants, and his pride.

Uncle Ed

Beneath a Ronald Reagan "Man of the Year" poster
and grandfather clock that bonged the hour,
he held court from the striped sofa.
Arms waving, Wild Turkey sloshing,
he'd argue and opine,
forever asking me to "ee-nun-cee-ate!"

In his heyday, he put up pickles
in crocks on the back porch,
sailed to Spain in a sloop,
skied Aspen and the Alps.

He centered the world
beneath the dining room's bead-and-wire mobile,
his family orbiting about, chattering and teasing,
until each one spun away, leaving him at the core
of the Mulberry Street homestead,
where nieces and nephews, grand and great-grand,
trekked for a dose of bric-a-brac.

Mother as a Young Woman

Before her face
fractured into wrinkles,
before ginger hair
and chile-pepper smile
turned to salt,
she'd walk that wire-
haired terrier anywhere,
both of them sniffing
low branches,
keen for novelty;

before she charmed
the loquacious Navy man,
before her body swelled,
then muscled me out,
before her back and jaw
pulled taut as rigging,
she looked like someone
I'd want to meet.

Maymont Park, 1961

It must be May,
    the azaleas
        a carnage
  on the walkway,
our mother's skirt   blown
      against obstinate legs,

my sister baring
    new teeth
    while Mother tightens
      her grasp   my sister
    clings   the air sick
      with sunshine.

Kiddie Pool, 1965

Five, I played Ring Around the Rosie
with neighbors who raced over,
kids with arms black as a wet street,
water beading their hair,
while my blonde curls turned stringy,
all fell down

when Grandmother slid open our screen,
stepped out, flowered hem bobbing
below knees, looked and gasped
as water rinsed off us, mixed together,
seeped into the lawn
where Mother calmly filled
a birdbath with the hose
and Father weeded tomatoes.

I thought she'd pinched her finger
slamming the door.

Father's Last Photo of His Girls

That morning, a robin hurtled
into the sliding glass door,
sagged by the hedge.
We sneaked out in slippers,
poked its feathers with a stick.
How do the dead feel?
Mother rushed out with a dishtowel.
Leave that poor thing alone!

Three days later,
Father's heart will shut down.
Mother will drive into "Emergency,"
carry home his watch and wallet.

When the snapshot comes back,
Father is reflected in glass sliders,
shoulders draped in a Sunday coat,
bowler covering his bald spot,
one eye closed, the other behind the camera,
forever composing us:

my sister and I upright on the picnic table,
stuffed bears wobbling on stocking-covered knees.

Mother as a Widow

In that garden
chair, it's all she can do to fill
her chest with air,
let it spill back out, used up.

What now of her hope
chest, stacked with linens?
The day they picnicked on the bluff
floated like yellow silk,

my father's arms a fine shawl,
the river whip-stitched
around rocks below,
grass blowing wild.

His faulty heart fusilladed
their promises,
shoveled dirt over
the rest of her life.

Swings at Humphrey Calder Park

Pointing the toe of her Ked in the dust,
there's my sister pushing off, rising up
after we abandoned the pick-up game
at the bottom of the third.
There was no reason to keep squinting
in the glare, while boys hogged the ball.

C'mon, she called, as I lagged back,
twisting in my swing.
Let's jump, she said. *It's easy.*
It's not.
Sure, it is. Watch!
Hair flapping, she rode the swing to its limit,
let go of the chains
to soar out, and land, laughing,
in tall grass by the fence.

The wind fanned my hair back,
tossed it across my cheeks.
I gasped as if plunging
underwater,
let go—
hurtled
past elm branches, shreds of
clouds, a church steeple tilted like
a speedometer in the red zone—
collided with the ground, elbow first.

The air stopped roaring.
The grass scratched.
I tried once, twice, three times to draw
a breath through my stuck chest.

Get up! she said. *Hey, get up!*
rolled me over with her foot.
Air rattled into my rib cage,
and my first sob escaped.
She wrapped her arms around me,
brown t-shirt rubbing my cheek,

wheeled my bike
out of the shrubbery and held it
while I climbed on.
Legs shaking, breath rasping,
I followed her into the street.

Photo Booth, 1974

After my father died, there was no one
to take my picture. Mother gave the family
camera, its springs and levers too baffling,
to Good Will. My hair tumbled
past her edict to keep it neat and trim,
into the hands of girls who wanted to feel
blonde. Nobody stepped up
to snap candids that cigarette-hazed year
there was no yearbook, no record
of elbows and spit. I wanted to see
more than a body widening
around a core of grief. I filled the instant
photo booth at Woolworth's with quarters
to capture what I was
becoming, balanced on a swivel
stool against the Formica wall,
stunned by the sudden strobe,
eyes glinting like stones.

PART IV

Second Time Around

                Let the dandelions
        turn gray, fly apart.

    It's time for thick towels,
  a wicker hamper,
          a new way to write my name.

                Loosening the drawstring waist
                        of mistakes, I am gaining
                velocity, volume,
            startling spin.

Urgent Spring

I want sun-spill,
roulette of clouds,

runaway mint to foam
on my worn-out tongue.

I want rattle of grass
to drown my lonely

as I reach past the moon,
pull down the dog

star, train him to sit,
stay by my feet.

How We Meet

Bundles of music leap
above the gong and clang,

my voice lilting while his
voice threads the room

like incense, spiraling up
through the shimmer

of sound until I whirl
with dust in the stage

lights, miss my cue,
lost, scanning the measures

until time starts again.

Amplified, My Son's Heart at 12 Weeks

rattles this curtained room
from its nest of splitting cells,
torque of the double helix,
clusters of buds and sockets

hammering back the silence
left the day my father's heart
strangled while I was on the sidewalk,
kicking slush on my way
home from school—

joy, a new and restless sound
battering inside me.

Out to Buy Milk

I want to see no farther than the road,
my windshield spattered with salt,
snowbanks slumped at the edges,
a red stutter of stop signs.

What I'm carrying is useless,
Kleenex and a butterscotch drop
that escaped from cellophane,
change rattling by the gearshift.

What I'm afraid to say trails
like exhaust: I'm staggering
under the weight of your smallness,
your serrated voice, your sticky

tracks up and down my arms,
your plastic animals, slimy
with drool, your hunger fishtailing
from blankets I lay gently on you.

My path is scraped clean
by plows, the distance like a picture
I once drew with too much white space,
the background filled with scribbles.

Twigs for Mother

I never thought I was a mother
who deserved my children—
warm heft of their miniature
hiccups, flailing arms, ruckus
of cries and ma-ma-ma,
the depth of *I trust you* to hold

leaves and acorns they bring me—
treasures I don't recognize.
I expected to keep treading
lonely gravel by the river,
fists clamped against privation
but my children call me

to the fallen nests of the world,
safety woven from twigs
carried high over the plagued city.
I cup in each palm the dirt
they scoop so carefully,
the offering of each shovelful.

Truth About Death

It really could happen any time—
close to the curb, at rush hour
when I walk my daughter to school,
or later, as I drive to work, the on-ramp
looping into a hiss of cars.

Nobody knows, I tell her
as I lie next to her at bedtime,
in the room where I felt the first twinge
of labor, her descent.

She covers my mouth with her fingers,
and I fall silent, trace the whorls
of her hair where it falls
across the clouds on her pajamas,
stroke the wings of her cheeks.

I Imagine My Son Leaving Home

Now he shuts his door, makes me knock.
Only when he sleeps can I take stealthy inventory,
the triumph of each lengthening bone.

His groggy, low-voiced *go away*
sounds like a strange man's in the house
and I wonder whose room I have stumbled into,
barefoot, in my bathrobe, as he holds up
one palm, luminous as a china pitcher, waving
away my dread, skateboard propped
against books of expired enchantment.

After My Mother's Hysterectomy

Gone is what confined me
while I was greedy
for light, for space, for the blessing
of my own breath—

it clunked inside you
ever since, a reminder
of how far you stretched,
how I damaged you.

When I got word from the receptionist
that you were comfortable
in recovery, I rushed
to the cafeteria for corn chowder,

something you'd never touch,
confetti of red peppers, kernels,
cayenne's incendiary flecks,
the bad calories of cream.

I fed myself
on a weatherworn bench,
sun bright, air cold,
grass aching with unrealized green.

My Father's Hometown

Charleston, West Virginia

I don't know my way down Quarrier or Kanawha,
streets he circled on his two-wheeler,
kid sister wobbling on handlebars,
twang in every conversation,
route to his old home a thicket of intersections,
no one there, anyway,
living room a travel agency.

If a clerk were keeping Sunday hours,
I would ask for a map of his heart,
trace switchbacks to the spot
where the arteries dead-ended
as I walked home from school,
whiskers from his morning shave
still littering the sink.

Concrete steps on his porch remain ordinary
as milk in glass bottles, for years
dropped off indifferently, the family
reading the *Gazette* at the breakfast table,
Grandmother's layer cake cooling
on the back porch. No place for me then,

no place for me now,
coal barges sloshing
the river that slices through town,
its surface faceted with sunlight,
my father flinging open the front door,
blonde buzz cut blazing
a swath clear to the mountains.

Loss

His face floated
away, a balloon
high over beech trees,
body thin as a vine.

From my embrace, he pulled
loose, lifted
into an ellipsis
trailing off in the wide sky,

leaving me mute,
hands empty,
grounded.

Father's Day

Take this threadbare grief:
fold it into a cardboard box,
tie black ribbon around it.

Place it on the high shelf,
the one I can't reach
without a stool.

Wrap the whole thing in plastic
in case it leaks onto my orange vest,
the one I wear running,

just to hear my heart,
always in danger of attack,
pounding through me like a timpani

as I raise the batons of my arms,
waving away time,
perspiration on my forehead, a balm.

PART V

Why Did You Move to Boston?

What's mine I built from squares and rotaries,
eyebrow windows and dovecotes. Striding in tough boots that stand
up to slush and salt. Lacerations of snow in my face. Servers rushing
through my coffee order. What's regular and what's not?

I wanted to leave languor, gouged-out war
trenches, the mansion my grandfather built and lost
to the bank. Schools that skewed the view
of history. Crape myrtle bark that peeled like scabs.

A blue line highlights the route I follow now, thicket
of roads and riverways. I can turn off, lose myself.

Where I Raised My Children

I know every invasive, every bulb with ruffled
purple fisted in its center, the rock
wall's shine of poison ivy,
and the willow, a spangled
cathedral for remains of our pets.

There's shelter under the forsythia, its splinters
of yellow each dreary
March, and the dogwood
that sprawls but never flowers.

The cedar now soars above
the window where my daughter greeted
a robin family, its babies quivering
with need, boughs cradling walls,
its trunk an old friend.

Outside the Boston Marathon Bomber Trial

Everyone's tweeting, tapping screens
in overworn winter coats.

City of sanctimony
given way to shrapnel,

a free fall of intolerance.
In the courthouse: his life,

his death. What will become
of the icy harbor, blue

pulse of patrol boats?
Water nibbles a shoreline

flanked by glass, a curtain
wall. Hatred and spectacle,

revolving gallery of justice:
Execution? Mercy?

Home, Shutdown

Marooned in a puddle
of windowpane sun, I long for

my work shoes drubbing brick
sidewalks. I miss bright streaks

of taxis and station-kiosk latte
foaming through the lid. I miss the dank

harbor dotted with vestiges
of ice harvesting and the China trade.

I'm stranded from the high-minded
Hub of the universe, its courthouse

carved with inspiration—*justice
is but truth in action.*

Now there are empty
boxes on the calendar,

April a storm in cherry
blossoms, bees gob-smacked by snow.

Making a Mask with My Mother's Sewing Kit

She left a needle already threaded
with black for a quick fix
of a rip, and a felt cushion

shaped like a heart, stuck with pins,
spools to match the only colors
she wore: navy, cream, plum.

I use her gold scissors to cut up
my t-shirt from a festival of twanging
music she never listened to,

stitch a rectangle to stifle
my breath. I follow the rules,
flatten the curve she escaped

which threatens to undo me.
She used to fit together
hems and seams, practical

and prepared, each stitch tallying
what I owed her, which could never
be enough. The mask hides the narrow

lips I inherited, the ones she kept
clamped. I try on the thimble, inhale
its brass smell. It won't protect me.

I Couldn't Protect My Sister

I tried to be for you the mother
we didn't have:
go to the doctor, send me the bill,
call me with the diagnosis.

What you needed was a hand,
to rub your shoulders, ease the velocity
of your hips always roaming
the rainbowed, out-of-reach city,
karma you couldn't reverse.

When you jumped,
it split me in two.
Half with you in heaven,
the other half fully on earth.

I never said goodbye
because I didn't know I'd have to—
an ordinary fall night, chill under my collar,
sneeze-spray of stars,
water a gleam,
then a wall.

Elegy for My Father

Just last week, our neighbor nailed
a red telephone with rotary dial
to a tree, invited
passersby to pick it up, listen
for voices of those
we had lost. I cradled
the plastic to my ear,
called my father, the number
remembered from when he taught me
what to do if I got lost.

That day I came home from second grade,
I told him, *and Mother said you were*
gone, I held
your pen, swallowed the water
in your green cup. I sat
on shoes in your closet,
reached for your sleeves.

After we moved, all I had left:
your red and black
checkered hunting jacket
barely warm enough day
after day at the school
bus stop I circled, hands
jammed in pockets, trying
to look tough.

After Visiting My Mother's Memorial Bench

Maymont Park, 2020

Down the slope, the park's pathways
begin. There, stinging
from recent widowhood, my mother turned
my sister and me loose through bamboo
thickets to a fountain where we plunged sticks
deep into algae-clumped pools.
No pennies for wishes. We all wanted
the same thing, anyway—my father
to walk back through the front door, whistling.

Today tulips, orange and yellow, dab
at the overcast sky as I approach
the colonnade, its dome a cupped hand,
our voices echoing like radio signals
lost in another star system.

A Calm Place

I swim through the golden
light of leaves reflected, the majesty
of branches above me. Churn in confident
rhythms—stroke, flutter, glide
through the province of mute
swans not yet migrated.
                                       In this season
of wild grapes, I take nourishment from tangled
ferment, turn my worried breath
into a spangled wake of bubbles.

April Storm

Allegro of rain
Waking up a vernal pool
Peepers: staccato

May Walk

In forest chartreuse
inhaling ferns and dampness
listen for warbling

On the Anniversary of My Father's Death

In the corner of my drawing, I crayon
the kind of sunshine a child
would want, all yellow rays,
and the brownish green river where geese
with goslings ply the murk, tender
and inscrutable. Water eddying
and flattening on its way to the harbor
in Boston. From the banks, spikes
of rotting reeds going back
to ooze. In the foreground, dragonflies
loop, strange and magical messengers.

Acknowledgments

Many thanks to the editors of the following publications in which these poems first appeared, sometimes in different versions, or with different titles:

Anthology of New England Writers, "Photo Booth, 1974," selected by Yusef Komunyakaa
Backchannels, "Where I Raised My Children"
Big Ugly Review, "My Father's Hometown"
Blackbird, "After Richmond Burned in 1865," "Out to Buy Milk"
Chautauqua, "If I Were Pocahontas Posing for My Portrait" "Twigs for Mother"
The Comstock Review, "In My Dark Days," "Father's Day"
Haiku Newton, "April Storm," "May Walk"
Haunted Voices, Haunting Places: An Anthology of Writers of the Old and New South, edited by Dr. Constantina Michalos (Halcyon Press), "Antebellum Biscuits," "Standard Drug Store," "Visiting the Confederate Trenches"
The Larcom Review, "The Starving Time"
Lumina, "Second Time Around"
The Mountains Anthology, edited by Margot Wizansky (Salt Marsh Pottery Press), "Tour of Capitol Square"
The Olive Press, "Family History," "Elegy for My Sister"
Paterson Literary Review, "Field Trip"
Pendemics Journal, "Making a Mask with my Mother's Sewing Kit"
Poetica and *Saying It Plain* (a Chautauqua literary annual)," "Whitewash on Concrete Walls"
Potomac Review, "Lake Anna"
Rhino, "Maymont Park, 1961" "High School Reunion"
The Sow's Ear, "Tourist in My Hometown"

*

I am grateful to Ruby Lee Norris and the Richmond Humanities Center for introducing me to contemporary poetry and nurturing me as a young writer. Thanks are also due to the Chautauqua Writers' Center, its founder and my mentor, Mary Jean Irion, and the many poets I worked with there, especially in my role as Program Director. Neil Shepard, Michael Waters, and Mihaela Moscaliuc provided helpful comments on early drafts of the manuscript. In Boston, I am grateful for the Workshop for Publishing Poets led by Barbara Helfgott Hyett, and the Poetry Round Table led by Grey Held. Grey also provided invaluable suggestions for this manuscript. Eric Hyett, Heather Nelson, and the entire Free Write group sparked some of the poems that appear in the book. Thanks also to writing colleagues Lee Hope, Meg Senuta, Faye Snider, and Robin Mayer Stein. My husband, George, and children, Jordan (who read and commented on many early drafts) and Martha, anchored me all along the way.

Clara Silverstein is the author of the memoir *White Girl: A Story of School Desegregation*, the historical novel *Secrets in a House Divided*, and four nonfiction books. Her poems have been nominated for a Pushcart Prize and have appeared at Boston City Hall and in *Blackbird*, the *Paterson Literary Review*, and other journals. Her articles and essays have been published in *Runner's World, Health* magazine, the *Boston Globe*, and several other publications. She has worked as a journalist, an historian, and Program Director of the Chautauqua Writers' Center. Raised in Richmond, Virginia, she now lives in Boston.

www.ingramcontent.com/pod-product-compliance
Lightning Source LLC
Chambersburg PA
CBHW030054170426
43197CB00010B/1517